Piano • Vocal • Guitar

twila paris
Where I Stand

ISBN 0-7935-6476-X

HAL•LEONARD™
CORPORATION
7777 W. BLUEMOUND RD. P.O. BOX 13819 MILWAUKEE, WI 53213

twila paris
Where I Stand

twila paris

Where I Stand

Hold On

Every little baby
Comes into the world
Reaching for an anchor
Fingers tightly curled
Grasping for a reason
Without knowing why
We will cling to anything
'Til the day we die

We can hold on to sorrow
Hold on to pain
We can hold on to anger
When there is nothing to be gained
We can hold to a thread
At the end of a rope
But if we hold on to Jesus
We are holding on to hope
Hold on
Hold on

This is human nature
This is what He planned
When He put our hearts inside
When He made these hands
We are here to reach for Him
Never letting go
This is all we need to have
All we need to know

And we can hold on to money
Hold on to fame
We can hold on to glory
And the honor of a name
We can hold to a thread
At the end of a rope
But if we hold on to Jesus
We are holding on to

Hold on to hope
Hold on to wisdom and grace
Hold on to mercy and love
Hold on

We can hold on to sorrow
Hold on to pain
We can hold on to anger
When there is nothing to be gained
We can hold on to money
Hold on to fame
We can hold on to glory
And the honor of a name
We can hold to a thread
At the end of a rope
But if we hold on to Jesus
If we hold on to Jesus
If we hold on to Jesus
We are holding on to hope

Hold on
Hold on
Go on
Hold on
Hold on

Love's Been Following You

I know sometimes it's hard to believe it
But Love's been following you
From where I stand I'm able to see it
And Love's been following you
All through the stormy night
Didn't you see the light
Goodness and mercy right there behind you
Love's been following you

Some days your heart just couldn't be colder
But Love's been following you
All you have learned just makes you feel older
But Love's been following you
You think that no one cares
Still Love is always there
He would go anywhere just to find you
Love's been following you

Love has been following you
Love's been following you
Love has been following you
Following you
Following you

Somehow the road just seems to get longer
But Love's been following you
Wait for the One who will make you stronger
'Cause Love's been following you
Wherever you go from here
Run far away from fear
Keep one thing very near and believe it's true
Love's been following you
Love's been following you
Love's been following you

Band of Survivors

Once more a remnant of the house of Judah
will take root below and bear fruit above.
For out of Jerusalem will come a remnant,
and out of Mount Zion a **band of survivors**.
The zeal of the Lord Almighty will accomplish this.
II Kings 19:30-31

This song is inspired by and dedicated to
the King's Kids of YWAM Arkansas who
consistently remind me that God will always
do great things through the energy and
innocence of a young heart that is given
completely to Him.

There is a war raging on
Between the right and wrong
And we have encountered the darkness
But as each night moves along
We face another dawn
To reach for the courage of love
As the faint hearted run for the shelter of home
There's a question that hangs in the air
When the smoke clears away from the battlefield
Who will be there

Will you stand with the band of survivors
Hand in hand
'Til the end of the day
Taking the land
With the band of survivors
Tried in the fire
Will you stand with the band

These are the ones
He will choose to win the victory
And He will declare it is over
And so we honor the call
Remain upon the wall
And trust in the name of our God
When the body is weak and the heart is afraid
Then be strong for the message is clear
When the banner is raised on the mountain
We still will be here

Will you stand with the band of survivors
Hand in hand
'Til the end of the day
Taking the land
With the band of survivors
Tried in the fire
Will you stand

Will you stand in the path of the strong man
To be counted for all you believe
Will you stand with the heart of a warrior
By the blood of the Lamb
In the name of the King

Will you stand with the band of survivors
Hand in hand
'Til the end of the day
Taking the land
With the band of survivors
Tried in the fire
Will you stand with the band
Will you stand with the band

Faithful Friend

Everyone knows you as a man of honor
I am glad to know you simply as a friend
You've always taken time to be my brother
And I'll be standing by you in the end

But I will never put you on a pedestal
I thank the Lord for everything you do
I'll be there to pray for you and for the ones you love
I believe that He will finish all He started in you

I will be an open door that you can count on
Anywhere you are, anywhere you've been
I will be an honest heart you can depend on
I will be a faithful friend

I am one of many whose path has been made clearer
By the light you've carried faithfully as a warrior
   and a child
God has used you greatly to encourage and inspire
And you've remained a true friend all the while

So I will never put you on a pedestal
'Cause we both know all the glory is the Lord's
And I'll be there to pray that He will keep you
   by His grace
And I always will remind you to be seeking His face

I will be an open door that you can count on
Anywhere you are, anywhere you've been
I will be an honest heart you can depend on
I will be a faithful friend

Should it ever come your time to mourn
I will weep with you
And every single time you win
I'm celebrating too
I will celebrate with you

I will be an open door that you can count on
Anywhere you are, anywhere you've been
I will be an honest heart you can depend on
I will be a faithful friend, I will be faithful
I will be a faithful friend

Jesus in You

The eyes are young
I won't deny it
But oh, the dream of tender youth
The seed is small
Do not despise it
Put on the robe and speak the truth
'Cause the only thing that matters
When the day has turned to night
Is a heart that knows the wonder
Of the mercy and the light

I can see Jesus in you
I see His love on your face
Go in His name and do all He commands you to do
I see Jesus in you

He brought you here
To build the kingdom
I see it burning in your eyes
The time is near
You must be ready
Do not be tempted by the lies
There is nothing that can hold you back
The wind has found the flame
You are called and you are chosen
You will never be the same

I can see Jesus in you
I see His love on your face
Go in His name and do all He commands you to do
I see Jesus
I see Jesus
I can see Jesus in you

I can see Jesus in you
I see His love on your face
Go in His name and do all He commands you to do
I see Jesus in you
I do
I see Jesus in you
I do
I see Jesus in you

Honor and Praise

Righteous and holy in all of Your ways
We come before You with honor and praise
Here to adore You for all of our days
We come before You with honor and praise

Lord of the heavens, how faithful You are
Shine down upon us, oh Bright Morning Star
Righteous and holy in all of Your ways
We come before You with honor and praise

Filling the temple, the work of Your grace
We come before You with honor and praise
Here to adore You for all of our days
We come before You with honor and praise

Lord of the heavens, how faithful You are
Rise in our spirits, oh Bright Morning Star

Righteous and holy in all of Your ways
We come before You with honor and praise
Here to adore You for all of our days
We come before You with honor and praise
Honor and praise
Honor and praise

Righteous and holy
We come before You
Righteous and holy
Honor and praise
Honor and praise
Honor and praise

I Am Not Afraid

I said I belonged to You
But in a secret room, I kept a secret list
I said, "Anything for You"
"Anything but this, anything but this"
You knew it all along
You knew it very well
You knew the sturdy walls I hid behind
Were nothing but a prison cell

I am not afraid anymore
You have opened all the windows
Opened all the doors
I am not afraid anymore
I feel the wind of freedom like I never did before
The light is filling up the corners
Dancing on the floor
I am not afraid anymore

You have always been the same
I ran away from You
I ran away from You
Every time You called my name
I tried to hide the truth
I tried to hide the truth
You knew it all along
You knew it very well
You knew the more I covered up my heart
The more I didn't know myself

I am not afraid anymore
You have opened all the windows
Opened all the doors
I am not afraid anymore
I feel the wind of freedom like I never did before
The light is filling up the corners
Dancing on the floor
I am not afraid anymore

No room for fear
No room, no room
No room for fear
Perfect love is living here

I am not afraid anymore
You have opened all the windows
Opened all the doors
I am not afraid anymore
I feel the wind of freedom like I never did before
The light is filling up the corners
Dancing on the floor
I am not afraid anymore
I am not afraid anymore
I am not afraid anymore
I am not afraid anymore

What Did He Die For?

He was twenty-one in 1944
He was hope and he was courage on a lonely shore
Sent there by a mother with love beyond her tears
Just a young American who chose to rise above
    his fears
And as I watch him struggle up that hill
Without a thought of turning back
I cannot help but wonder

What did he die for?
When he died for you and me
Made the sacrifice
So that we could all be free
I believe we will answer each to heaven
For the way we spend a priceless liberty
Look inside and ask the question
What did he die for?
When he died for me

To the darkest day in A.D. 33
Came the mercy and compassion of eternity
Sent there by a Father with love beyond His tears
Blameless one, the only Son to bear the guilt of
    all these years
And as I watch Him struggle up that hill
Without a thought of turning back
I cannot help but wonder

What did He die for?
When He died for you and me
Made the sacrifice
So that we could all be free
I believe we will answer each to heaven
For the way we spend a priceless liberty
Look inside and ask the question
What did He die for?

He died for freedom
He died for love
And all the things we do to pay Him back
Could never be enough

What did He die for?
When He died for you and me
Made the sacrifice
So that we could all be free
I believe we will answer each to heaven
For the way we spend a priceless liberty
Look inside and ask the question
What did He die for?
When He died for me

House of Cards

One by one
We climb the mountain of ambition
One by one
And we bow at the altar of tradition
One by one
Somebody tell me what are we building

You know the house of cards will tumble
Temporary by design
And all the schemes of man will crumble
Are we wasting precious time
Are we wasting precious time

Stone by stone
We build a kingdom to perfection
Stone by stone
And we search for our safety and protection
In a home
Somebody tell me what are we thinking

You know the house of cards will tumble
Temporary by design
And all the schemes of man will crumble
Are we wasting precious time

When there is only one Kingdom
One place to hide
Only one Kingdom
Come and find a place inside
Come and find a place inside
Come and find a place inside

Because a house of cards will tumble
Temporary by design
And all the schemes of man will crumble
Are we wasting precious time
Are we wasting precious time
Are we wasting precious time
Are we wasting precious time

I Never Get Used to What You Do

I look on the outside
You look on the heart
Where I see an ending
You can see another place to start
And every time I see Your hand reach down
I know a lonely child has just been found

But I never get used to what You do
I never get used to watching You
Take a life beyond redemption
Make it yours and make it new
I never outgrow the miracle
A heart that was empty flowing full
I never get used to what You do

I grew up surrounded by
The Family of Life
You'd think I would know by now
You'd think I would never be surprised
But every time it takes my breath away
And I think it is time You heard me say

I never get used to what you do
I never get used to watching you
Take a life beyond redemption
Make it Yours and make it new
I never outgrow the miracle
A heart that was empty flowing full
I never get used to what You do ·

Father of grace and love without end
God of forgiveness, Faithful Friend
Every time I see Your hand reach down
Another lonely child has just been found
Every day Your mercy is brand new
And we would all be lost if not for You

I never get used to what You do
I never get used to watching You
Take a life beyond redemption
Make it Yours and make it new
I never outgrow the miracle
A heart that was empty flowing full
I never get used to what You do
I never get used to what You do

I Will Listen

Hard as it seems
Standing in dreams
Where is the dreamer now
Wonder if I
Wanted to try
Would I remember how
I don't know the way to go from here
But I know that I have made my choice
And this is where I stand
Until He moves me on
And I will listen to His voice

This is the faith
Patience to wait
When there is nothing clear
Nothing to see
Still we believe
Jesus is very near
I can not imagine what will come
But I've already made my choice
And this is where I stand
Until He moves me on
And I will listen to His voice

Could it be that He is only waiting there to see
If I will learn to love the dreams that He has
    dreamed for me
Can't imagine what the future holds
But I've already made my choice
And this is where I stand
Until He moves me on
And I will listen to His voice

LOVE'S BEEN FOLLOWING YOU

Words and Music by
TWILA PARIS

HOLD ON

Words and Music by
TWILA PARIS

on, _____ hold _____ on. _____

rit.

BAND OF SURVIVORS

Words and Music by
TWILA PARIS

FAITHFUL FRIEND

Words and Music by TWILA PARIS
and STEVEN CURTIS CHAPMAN

Female: Ev - 'ry - one knows ____ you as a man ____ of hon - or. I am glad ____ to know _____ you simply as ____ a friend. ____ You've al - ways tak - en

I CAN SEE JESUS IN YOU

Words and Music by
TWILA PARIS

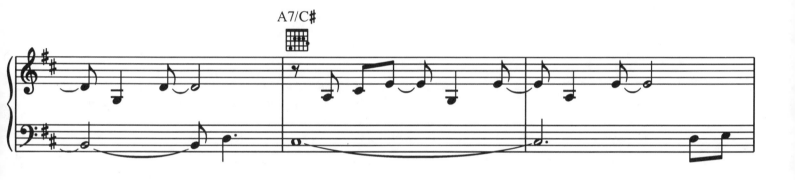

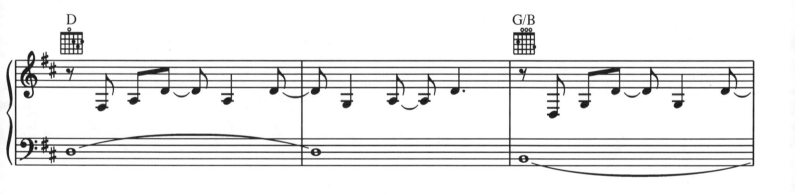

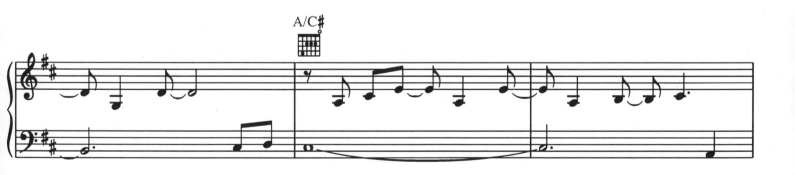

44

HONOR AND PRAISE

Words and Music by
TWILA PARIS

I AM NOT AFRAID

Words and Music by
TWILA PARIS

I said I_____ be - longed _____ to You, _____ but in a
You have al - ways been _____ the same. _____ I ran a -

WHAT DID HE DIE FOR?

Words and Music by
TWILA PARIS

64

HOUSE OF CARDS

Words and Music by
TWILA PARIS

Are we wast - ing pre - cious time?

Are we wast - ing pre - cious time?

Repeat and Fade

I NEVER GET USED TO WHAT YOU DO

Words and Music by
TWILA PARIS

I WILL LISTEN

Words and Music by
TWILA PARIS

Hard as it seems,
This is the faith;

stand - ing in dreams,
pa - tience to wait

where is the dream -
when there is noth -

- er now? ___
- ing clear. ___

86